My Father, in Snow

MY FATHER, IN SNOW

E. Sheila Johnson

To Bill and Rita —

So happy any heartful
families found each other
in this world —

with love,

Sheila 2.7.15

9 × 2 Press

Nine by Two Press

Madison, Connecticut

ninebytwopress@gmail.com

Visit us at myfatherinsnow.com

ISBN:

hardcover 978-0-9905912-1-4

trade paperback 978-0-9905912-0-7

e-book 978-0-9905912-2-1

Library of Congress Control Number: 2014914307

First edition

Book edited and designed by Kevin M. Johnson.

Front cover photograph © Jonathan E. Chen, used with permission under

Creative Commons BY-SA license.

Printed in the United States of America

To my mother and father
who taught us
the meaning of joy

Contents

Foreword

My sister Sheila's beautiful manuscript in remembrance of our father sat hidden in her files for many years. She has permitted me to help her prepare it as the centerpiece of this book. In it, she conveys the warmth, confusion, and longing of a young girl who loved her father, and lost him too soon.

Interspersed with Sheila's remembrances are transcriptions of interviews with our brothers and sisters. The intention is to preserve the rhythms of their speech; therefore, their memories have been only lightly edited and are otherwise verbatim. These sections are best read as though listening to someone speaking.

In the epilogue, I have myself written an account of our father's train ride home from work one evening. His imagined reverie hews to actual events as recounted by my mother to my brother Brian, and in a letter to her from our father.

My sister Nancy, the eighth of his nine children, who was very young when he died, had this to say: "I remember Dad through stories other people told about him. His sister

Aunt Anne talked a lot about him. She was very close to him and protective of him. We were up there one time for her birthday. Our brother Bob was talking to her about him and asking specific questions. It was the first time—and this sounds weird—where I thought of Dad as a real person, if that makes any sense. I had heard about Dad, I had heard about this Dad, that he was really great and loving and all these different things. But it was the first time—I was what, 35 years old at the time?—that he became real."

My hope is that through this book, Dad will become real to another generation. And perhaps his story will help other readers conjure memories of their own beloved, and never to be forgotten, fathers.

Kevin Johnson
Madison, Connecticut
September 2014

The Johnson Children

Cathy

Bob

Sheila   the "big kids"

Jack

Kevin

Marian

Brian   the "little kids"

Nancy

Eileen

Prologue

I have no father. Of course, I had one. But not now—not for a long time. I have operated my life in this vacuum, inventing a father. Recasting the pieces, I remember a father of my own imagining. He is not real, this father I make. He does not breathe or talk to me or hold me safely to console me as I would want a father to do. He is not warm and quick.

How could he die in the middle of my adolescence—the two of us battling out independence and my femininity? Boys or no boys? Dates or no dates? Traveling in cars or no cars? Lingering in the porch light for a kiss or no kiss from some boy I barely remember. My father within, flicking the light.

What is it like when all is right with a father? How do women change in years of conversations and moments with him—of going away and returning? Does the bond deepen? Does the bond break? What do women learn of themselves and of men? How does this long relationship with a father inform the love a woman feels for a husband?

I have no way to know. Women with less than perfect real fathers cannot imagine, need not imagine such a father as mine. They wrestle and reckon with a real person. I reckon with legend and dream.

Chapter 1

ELYRIA, OHIO

Each time my mother went to the hospital to have a baby, my father would take us over in the evening with him to visit her. We couldn't go in, being children, but he'd leave us on the green where there were tall trees and a great hill to roll down, after pointing to the window on the floor where she was and then we'd watch the window for them both to appear.

They were so far away, so high in the window, two figures pressed against each other in the glass. I'd look hard to see my mother's face, or to see if that really was a baby in her arms. At times, I doubted that I was looking up at the right window. They seemed so far away. At the bottom of the hill on that green, we waved, wishing my mother could come home with us and not leave anymore, looking in her arms for this new little stranger who would soon make us all stare at their tininess. And when my father would come down, he would wave to her, and I was assured it was the right window we had been watching.

How hard it was for him to turn to leave her even knowing she'd soon be home. He'd turn and turn again. He'd get in the car with all of us and drive once again past that side of the building for another glance of this woman and the tiny new creature she had just delivered into his life.

Nine children arrived in 17 years: first Cathy, then Bob, Sheila, Jack, Kevin, Marian, Brian, Nancy, and the youngest, Eileen. My father once said he hoped to have 12. Close enough.

He would leave his tie on for dinner. If hot, he'd roll up the starched white sleeves of his shirts that had come from the dry cleaners in blue cardboard boxes. On Saturdays he would wear a short-sleeve cotton shirt, light plaid or, in winter, a rust-colored corduroy.

He was tall, six feet at least, lean with large hands and long arms beneath a gold watch he always wore. He had glasses with gold wire rims, then dark horn rims later. Usually he wore a white shirt and a tie that was striped or polka-dotted and sometimes even a bowtie, with gray, brown or navy suits. He always had lots of change and keys that jingled when he came down the steps into the living room. He had dark hair that later got gray with one white stripe streaked to the right of center, hair he combed straight back on top, the sides clipped short with little gray strands that brushed by with his whiskers when he hugged you. Going for haircuts with him was one of our big Saturday excursions.

He had blue eyes, very blue, sea blue, quick kind eyes, curious and thoughtful, quick-to-smile blue eyes. He had some lines on his face but not many, most where he would raise one eyebrow about something one of us was doing—it was enough. He had full lips, smiling a tiny bit more to the right than left and a cleft in his chin that even had whiskers in it. He definitely had tough whiskers that added mystery to his goodnight kiss; we watched him shaving with a Gillette razor, wondering why fathers had these bristly faces when otherwise they seemed so soft.

He wore big overcoats and hats. Also, I think he wore boxer shorts with little red diamonds or blue paisleys that I would notice when I carried the laundry up and folded it on the dining room table.

He always carried a handkerchief in his back pocket, which he brought home one day bloodied when a child on a bicycle had been hit by a car and Dad was a witness. He held the hankie over the child's injuries until help arrived. He told us about this at dinner in the kitchen. It was one of our more somber meals. I don't recall if the child died or if our father told us of the extent of the injuries, only his own sadness when he spoke of seeing this occur. Then for a few moments he was silent, sitting bent over his food in front of the high white kitchen cupboards.

Usually, after saying grace, Dad would ask everybody about their day at school, what they learned today. It took a lot of concentration to engage in this exchange while making sure you got enough meat and mashed potatoes. The food came in big white bowls that seemed endless until they were passed to my brothers. We had regular seats based on practical considerations of who needed help cutting meat or being fed or who could go it on their own. Mom sat at one end and Dad at the other. I was second from Dad on his right; first was someone smaller like Kevin who needed Dad's help with tough food problems. Mom had a baby in a high chair to her left and a little person like Marian to her right. My parents would look at each other from the ends across three, five, seven, eventually nine small plates. They would do in a look what I would later struggle years to achieve with another human being.

In our dining room there was a piano, a bassinet, a huge china closet, a table with seating for eleven, a burgundy carpet, and two big windows with striped drapes that looked out to a yard with a pear tree. Beneath the windows, lilies of the valley grew each summer and snowdrifts came up to the windowsill one winter.

Mostly I remember how I felt when I was around him: good, safe, like an adventure might develop at any moment, but also respectful of his authority and his expectation of our good behavior, our honesty, academic seriousness, and helpfulness towards Mom.

Robert Edward Johnson was born in 1913 in Drifton, near Hazleton, Pa., the fifth child of John Joseph Johnson Jr. and Mary Ann Reilly Johnson. He had two brothers and three sisters. Young Jack, the firstborn, died of complications of a severe birth injury said to have been caused by forceps—he was bedridden from birth and just seven years of age when he died. My father came along several years later.

Dad's father was the above-ground superintendent for the local coal colliery. He was known for being the first Irish "boss" in a region that had for many years practiced the "no Irish need apply" rule. He was well-respected for being fair and even-handed, beloved by workers and kind to their families, especially during crises.

Dad's grandfather, John Joseph Sr., was a local poet and songwriter in a time and place where men with such talents were a principle source of entertainment. But at the same time he was a coal miner, as was his father before him, until the Spanish flu epidemic of 1918 claimed him.

My father's family had been given a large company house and property that included a garden and the services of a gardener and other household help. They even built a small swimming pool. Bob and his brother Leonard were enterprising, charging the neighbor children admission to movies in the garage and to the pool in summer. They led a life of privilege compared to many of their peers.

Some summers, we would drive to Pennsylvania in our '57 Chevy station wagon, me sitting right behind Dad on the Scotch cooler. It was a rather cool hard seat but at a window and so close to him that I could reach forward and feel the soft salt and pepper hair on his head if I wanted to. The breeze through the open windows blew our hair, and we felt we were on some exotic adventure, coming through tunnels and over mountains at night. We would beg him to rouse us if we were sleeping when he reached a certain point on Route 309 just before our destination:

"Wake us up to see the lights of Hazleton!"

Logistics

CATHY

When we were buying the station wagon—it was maybe the first real new car Mother and Dad ever bought—we all went and tried to fit into all these cars. And we wound up getting this kind of funny-colored golden yellow station wagon. We were all so thrilled; otherwise we would all have been squished into a sedan. That was a big time.

BOB

Each summer, the whole family would take a trip back to Hazleton and Freeland, Pa., to see Dad's and Mom's families. There would be so much to pack in terms of clothes and all the rest. At least one year he took the measurements inside the trunk and then he created boxes that fit the measurements of the trunk. They were rounded and so forth so that when he was done the whole of the trunk was one big box. All the volume of the trunk was used up. He built the boxes himself somehow.

Then we'd all be jammed in the car. In the back seat there would be, I don't know, six of us or something. Back then—that was before the turnpike—we would take a toll road in Ohio, but once we hit the middle of Pennsylvania we were on the regular roads. It was a long drive. Then we would look for the lights of Hazleton.

KEVIN

He had all these kids in the car, and it was a long trip. So one of his innovations was to carry an empty peanut butter jar in the back seat. That was for Brian and me to use as needed to relieve ourselves. We were very small then. I guess he still had to stop for all the girls, but it cut down the stops by some percentage. Dad was practical like that.

MARIAN

Just imagine fitting all these people in the car. It just was crazy. But my favorite was if I got to sit in the middle in the front because that meant I got to sit between my Mom and my Dad; my Dad always drove and my Mom would be holding somebody. So there were four people just in the front now. Then you'd layer the rest into the back. I liked it when it was nighttime—it just had a safe feeling. Everybody was quiet, I guess that's why, and I could just lean on my Dad or lean on my Mom and we would just be driving, driving. And every now and then he would point things out. It was just very serene, very serene.

Chapter 2

CASCADE PARK

Money was not endless. We rented rather than owned a house in Elyria. There was certainly no gardener and no swimming pool. Ours was a modest two-story frame house with a small front porch on the corner of Dewey Avenue and Madison Street, one block from St. Agnes Catholic Church and one block from the elementary school. Someone once counted 53 children living on our square block; a family across the street had 14 children alone.

My father was always working. He was away so much that the prospect of his return always sent a thrill through us.

We would wait many nights at 6 p.m. like puppies lined up on the curb for Dad to come down Dewey Avenue in his green '51 Plymouth sedan with the plush gray upholstery, the seats higher than my head, the windows large and breezy.

We would wait—my brothers, sisters, assorted neighbor kids, and sometimes kids it seemed we hardly knew—for my father to start down the hill at the top of our street.

He would turn off Lake Avenue from his job in Lorain or Cleveland, probably tired, probably worn out. Still he'd gather us up, child, neighbors and friends and take us for one ride around the block, maybe two. Once we went all the way out to the country. He got a flat tire, and all the kids had to go to the bathroom. All their parents were holding dinner for them, and one other father got really mad.

In the summer, often we would persuade him to take us to Cascade, the town park, the ultimate destination. Pleading time, he sometimes said no. But he loved adventure as much as we; indeed, he taught us to seek it in the simplest ways. So usually he said yes. Everyone cheered and clapped, sang songs, whistled, and tumbled over each other's legs in a back seat celebration. Then *"shhh…"* someone would say, all quiet, all of us settling ourselves, preparing for the ritual: the descent into the great green park where the Black River ran over big flat rocks that the Black River Indians used to stand on, vigilant, still.

There were three or four entrances to the park. The best one was the furthest away. The road curved past houses, then by a big brown sign became steep, turning down through tall trees in a spiral. At that point, we'd brace and all dip down into the park, our arms straddling the open windows, two or three faces at each one, others settling back against the plush gray seat, watching the green branches twirl by the light through the trees, the leaves, the moisture from the ravine rising up in our throats, following the road along the river by the places we had picnics, at tables and barbecue pits under trees, along the river that was so green, so deep, so dangerous to go to without permission or parents.

The road continued along the big rocks, old, initialed, past the smell of chlorine from the pool where I took beginner's lessons three times, the sledding hill, the baseball fields, the smells from the bears in their cages up the path from the swings, those big smelly black bears in cages under rocks that my father liked to see. Sometimes he would let us sit on the rocks by the river and look at the light on the water. Sometimes he took our picture there. Often he would stop the car at the playground. We would scatter like unnetted birds to roost on the swings and slides, set in sand that would come home with us in our clothes.

Stopping there was okay, but I preferred to keep moving with him in the car, through the park, amid the soft green trees. It was as if the car had no motor, gliding effortlessly, smoothly, carried by the breeze through the windows. He, often quiet, thinking perhaps about the day, unwinding; and although there were many of us in the car and it was full of children's voices, laughter, small disputes, it all seemed so orderly, so joyful, each of us respectful of this privilege, to be part of this adventure, this evening mission.

At the deepest point of the park the road forked. One path continued straight ahead; the other turned left across a low concrete path under the Black River. Not a bridge, but a ford.

When the water at the river was not too high, they would open the ford and we, given time, would cross in my father's car, his great green car traversing the great green river, slowly, slowly, I clutching the seat, sitting behind him, eyes fixed on the back of his head, or beside him leaning into his arm as he negotiated the steering wheel, water rushing over the ford, our wheels cutting slowly through the water. Only in his car I thought, could I, would I ever want to do this, safe in the interior, him, talking to me, knowing he would never do anything to harm me. I trusted him, his ability to figure things out, the wheels still cutting through the water, slowly, slowly, sunlight glimmering on the river and glancing off his glasses. My father, after all, was an engineer. He was good at everything. He was smart. And when we came up finally, our tires rolling up the other bank out of the river onto the road, the whole car cheered, and I breathed at last and pried my head out from under his arm where I had wedged it and he had permitted me to do so.

And we would rise up, out through the other side of the park, where the town's first families had lived, their long yards and big white houses stretching down a great wide street toward home where my mother had dinner waiting.

Playfulness

JACK

One time we were going to Cascade Park, the car was full of kids, and Dad was in entertainment mode. Once you entered the park, you went down this winding road, a hill going down, because it was in a big ravine. At some point about halfway down—the car is going about 20 miles per hour max—he says, "Well, it's time for me to get out of here." So he opens the door and puts one foot as though he is stepping out. Of course, everybody goes "Oh no, no!" He closes the door, a big smile on his face. He was quite satisfied with himself. And Mom was looking at him with daggers. Which is exactly how my wife Midge looked at me when I tried to do it one time.

KEVIN

Dad used to like to take us for ice cream. That was always one of his big evening activities with us. He would come into the living room or wherever, pause, look around a little, and announce, "Who wants to go see the old man with the whiskers?" and with that we would all scramble out the door to the car. I think the whiskers he referred to were the whipped cream on sundaes, though Marian remembers an actual old man with actual whiskers at the shop.

MARIAN

When he would come home from trips he'd have his big suitcase. You always knew there was a brown bag in there full of candy bars. We'd patiently wait until he would take his suitcase upstairs—and sometimes he'd pretend he didn't have anything, you know, that kind of thing. But he would take out all the candy bars and he would have just enough for however many kids there were and he would dump them on the floor. We'd cry, "Oh my gosh, candy bars!" He pretty much knew what people liked. Sometimes he'd put them behind his back and make you guess, but somehow he always managed it so that you got the one you wanted. Sometimes instead he would take money in each hand and you would have to guess how much was in each hand—because our brother Bob used to do that then later on. I think Dad would switch up the change in his hand because at first you wouldn't have enough for a candy bar, but then he'd make sure you did.

KEVIN

He was promising to help me make a crystal radio. This is a radio that doesn't have a battery, it just has a little crystal and coil of wire, and you string a big long wire out the back to the garage and you can receive radio signals. So he kept saying he was going to bring stuff home for that. He was always extremely busy; that's why everybody remembers these moments with him because they were not that frequent.

So one day after work he was sitting in the kitchen with my mother and I came in and asked, "Dad, did you bring the wood home?"—he was going to bring a piece of wood home for the base—and he said, "Oh, I forgot again, I'm sorry."

But my mother somehow signaled that perhaps this was not the case. I started looking around and found the board behind the door to the basement. But we never had a chance to build the radio.

SHEILA

When I had just turned 7 and my sister Cathy 11, my parents had a joint birthday party for us in the backyard. There must have been 50 kids, and I think it was to make up for missing our birthdays because my Mom had been in the hospital. My father had organized potato races, softball, and croquet, and lots of other activities in the backyard.

I felt a little overwhelmed. I remember thinking this must cost a bunch of money. So I disappeared for a while with my girlfriend Ginger to sit on the front porch steps to look at the grass growing.

My father came searching for me.

"What's wrong?" he said.

"Nothing", I said. "Just too much going on."

"Oh. Okay," he said.

There are photos he snapped of the potato races on that day and the lovely cakes and gifts, but my favorite is the one he took of just me and Ginger sitting on the front steps in our party dresses, watching the grass grow.

BRIAN

I remember him reciting "The Night Before Christmas." This would have been all of the little kids, sitting there listening. He would say, "'Twas the night before Christmas and all through the house not a creature was stirring not even a MOOSE." We would laugh and I'd laugh especially hard and I remember overdoing it, laughing really hard and falling down on my back because I wanted him to know that I thought this was great.

KEVIN

On Christmas Eve, he would put up the bare tree and the board for the train, but there would be absolutely nothing else. Then he and Mother would stay up all night and when we'd get up the next morning the tree would be decorated, the lights would be on, the trains would be up and running, all the toys would be out. Each kid had his or her own "pile." The toys would, however, not be wrapped. That's the explanation for my own kids why presents from Santa Claus are not wrapped.

About 20 years later, I visited our old neighborhood in Elyria and ran into the next-door neighbor shoveling his walk. He volunteered that he remembered seeing the lights stay on all Christmas Eve in our house. I stood there on the sidewalk with him—it was late afternoon—and looked up at the windows of our old house and tried to imagine those lights.

KEVIN

On Easter mornings it was mandatory to stay upstairs until everybody was ready to go down together. But one Easter, as we gathered with Mother at the top of the stairs, we saw Dad wandering around down in the living room all disheveled, in his dressing gown and slippers with his hair mussed, acting a little confused.

We shouted at him, "Dad, what are you doing! You're not supposed to be down there! It's Easter!"

"I must have fallen asleep on the couch last night."

This was something he had never actually done.

"This morning I heard noises and jumped up and saw somebody or something running out the front door. Come down and look!"

So we all ran down and there was a trail of candy from the living room out into the front yard. Of course, we were all thrilled and amazed. It was magical.

A couple of years later when one of my classmates tried to tell me that Santa Claus was not real, I countered that my Dad had seen the Easter Bunny, and if he was real, Santa Claus wasn't so much of a stretch.

Chapter 3

KIDS, BIG AND LITTLE

From the start, I learned that life was something to be shared, not one person's exclusive property. As the third child, the world I entered already had others in it, and although my voice was heard, it was part of a chorus, joined by six more over the next 11 years.

Babies, lots of children, many voices, only so many cupcakes, so that separating what was mine and what was not mine was daily business. Much of it I don't remember, but this life in community, this thriving metropolis that was our house left its imprint. Indeed, it formed me.

It was not exactly a democracy, but everyone had rights, and my father ruled as king, or sort of benevolent dictator, sergeant, or maybe just a good boss, managing all of our personalities as he did the engineers at the Magic Chef Stove

Company. I hope they found his supervision as fair, usually, as did I. He never had to do more than raise his voice slightly above normal or turn suddenly and stiffen his shoulders so that the blue in his eyes deepened and we knew.

There was a time or two I talked back to my mother, the only indiscretion I recall that really brought forth his anger— doing anything disrespectful toward my Mom, my beautiful mostly always pregnant Mom.

We thought pregnancy was her normal state. At the time, I didn't know my father had anything to do with that; I thought God on His own gave us babies. The only thing I knew my father did was treat her like the most beloved, rare presence in his life. When he'd come home from work or an errand, there was a way he kissed her, as if glad she was still there, as if she might disappear at any moment. He talked to her every night long after we went to bed.

There were babies being soaped and rinsed and twirled in towels at the kitchen sink. Small children running in pajamas with feet, flannel with little animals in the winter, seersucker dots in the summer, all with connecting snaps that strained under the bulk of cloth diapers and rubber pants.

On the back porch, he put in shelves and a file cabinet from work to organize our toys. We each got one shelf and one drawer for skates and balls and dolls and collected rocks.

He drew us together for meetings to discuss helping Mom with household chores and earning our allowances.

We were always given the money we needed for school, Scouts, and so forth, but for recreational funds he believed in the incentive program. Jobs around the house were given a point assignment and every five points equaled a penny. Babysitting earned 50 points or 10 cents an hour; dishwashing was good for 35 points or 7 cents a sinkful. Those with ambition or a special purchase in mind could work like whirlwinds for a few days.

It was a great motivator, especially for my brother Bob who took the worst jobs like ironing, washing dishes, and scrubbing the kitchen floor because they had the highest points-to-pennies ratio. The only thing higher was babysitting because it entailed the most responsibility. That's the one I picked. I was good at it, or at least I worked at developing a reputation in that area.

Still, we got all we asked for at Christmas, and new dresses for Holy Communion and Confirmation, and special outfits for summer vacations.

My father's response to the potential chaos that hung over a family with all those kids was organization and "Let's do this together." There were little kids and there were big kids. Anyone over the age of 7 was considered to have reached the age of reason and therefore capable of looking out for someone

smaller. These big kid-little kid matchups my father called
our "charges." It made us feel important and responsible. It
meant that if you were a big kid, at all times you should look
out for, tag after, or shepherd about your little charge. The
oldest kid got the youngest kid. My sister Cathy's charge was
Brian. Bobby had Marian, and Kevin was mine. My mother
took care of the baby who at that time was Nancy. I think
Jack was in charge of himself, which was a fairly demanding
assignment in those days.

On Saturdays we'd all work. Then we'd all play. What
confession and the drive-in have in common I don't know
except that on Saturday after we had walked up to St. Agnes
to confession, a weekly or bi-weekly practice, my Dad occasionally got the idea that after that we'd all go to the drive-in.
Everyone, all the kids that is, would put on their pajamas.
Then we would pile into the station wagon. Going to the
movies in your pajamas seemed like a crazy thing to do, but
it made it easier when later, much later, after popcorn and
sodas and Hershey bars in the dark, my father would carry
each one of us over his shoulder in from the car up to bed.
He must have been very optimistic to have had all those kids,
confident in the future.

One summer, it was much harder, for we would go to the
green with him and he'd go up to see my mother, but she
would not come to the window and there was no new baby

and it lasted a long time. She had ulcerative colitis. I didn't know what that was except that she almost died from it that summer. My father finally had to ask relatives in Hazleton and Freeland and Philadelphia to take all of us for the summer. Cathy went with my aunt on a plane to Philadelphia with the babies, Brian and Marian, where my aunts cared for them. Jack, Bob, Kevin and I went to my grandmother's in Hazleton and my mother's family in Freeland. At my grandmother's I wrote a letter:

> *Dear Mom and Dad,*
>   *I hope things are better than when we left. Dad, it*
> *must seem funny your being there alone. When it's quiet*
> *here it just doesn't seem right either...*
> *Love,*
> *Sheila*

I told them how when we arrived at Aunt Mary Ellen's house Kevin refused to enter and started screaming to go home and Uncle John and he had to sleep on a park bench all night instead. I'm sure that made them feel much better.

At the end of the summer, those of us in school came home. My mother had recovered and was resting upstairs. The evening we arrived, quietly tiptoeing in, it seemed so still in the house. My father went up and escorted her down the staircase. She was like a thin, pale young girl, fragile, having lost so much weight, having almost died someone said. My mother was all right now. Later she told us that she had to eat a lot of rice to get better. The colitis returned from time to time in small bouts and then seemed to leave her.

She had Nancy a year and a half after that, and Eileen a year and a half after that.

Psychology

BRIAN

The other thing Mom said about Dad was what a psychologist he was. What she meant was he understood psychology in dealing with people. She said he was the best person at handling children of anybody she had ever seen.

JACK

When I was 10, I think we were in Elyria, Dad pulled me aside one time and said, "So are any of your friends smoking yet?" I was looking at him like I had no idea what he was talking about. I said, "Oh no—what?—no!" He said, "Okay, well one of these days one of your friends will come and say, 'Hey, you want to have a smoke, you want to smoke a cigarette with me?'" And he said, "When that time comes, I want you to come to me, and I will show you how to do it right, so you don't get sick or anything." And I said, "Oh okay," and that was it. Within about two, three years, kids were starting to smoke, and one of my friends came and said, "Hey, do you want to have a smoke?" and I said, "Oh no, my dad's going to show me how, he said he'd train me." There was no mystery, zero, none. There was no like, 'Hey I'm going to sneak this,' because I felt like—I didn't realize what was going on, the psychology—I thought, I can smoke anytime I want. And it worked like a charm. I never did smoke.

JACK

I was 7, 8, 9, somewhere in there. Mom would bring out dinner family style, on the platters, and we would take stuff and put it on our plates. She said, "Everybody take at least one beet. I want everybody to have one." Mom was always having us try different vegetables, not just potatoes.

So I didn't ask for the beet, but I got it. And it was literally a round-shaped ball the size of a small tennis ball. I didn't like beets, I didn't like the way they smelled, I didn't know much about how they tasted because they smelled so bad to me. So we're sitting there and everybody is eating and all the other people eat their beet. I eat everything else. The beet is still on my plate.

Mom says, "Well, we have dessert."

Dad said, "Jack, you need to eat that beet."

And I said, "But I don't like beets."

"That's okay, it's good for you. Why don't you try it?"

"Oh no, I don't want to eat this beet."

Dad said to Mom, "What do you have for dessert?"

"I have ice cream, vanilla ice cream."

"Okay, why don't you serve it."

She looked at me, then looked at him.

"Should I do it yet, because Jack didn't eat the beet?"

And I remember he said, "Oh yeah, bring it out, bring out the ice cream, including for Jack!"

It was a test of wills.

So Mom brings out the ice cream. And everybody else has their ice cream. I'm sitting there and the ice cream is in front of the plate with the beet on it, and I'm not eating the beet.

Dad said, "You can't have the ice cream until you eat the beet."

And I looked at him like, "Oh yeah?"

So I sat there. The other kids finished their ice cream, got up and left. I'm still sitting there with the beet and the melting ice cream. Dad finally gets up from the table and says "Do not eat the ice cream until you eat that beet. Don't do it."

And Mom is looking a little regretful, because she was the one who wanted everybody to eat the beet.

So he goes off into the next room, and I'm sitting there staring at it and staring at it. This goes on for like 15 minutes. The ice cream is just about all melted. And finally I turned to Mom—because she was watching over me—and I said, "Could I have a large glass of milk?" And she says, "Sure," and comes back with the milk. I take the glass of milk in one hand and my fork in the other and I stab the beet and I literally stuff it in my mouth and I chug the milk. I almost swallowed the beet whole. So then I could have my ice cream. But he was pretty tough that way, and I got the message.

BRIAN

One time when he came home Mom was really at her wit's end with the kids and everything and he said, "You should go to the movies." He called her a cab and gave her whatever it cost and sent her to the movies by herself, because there wasn't somebody he could call to come watch the kids right then. It was a Tuesday or Wednesday night. I asked her what she did and she said, "Well, I went to the movies." It gave her a chance to get a break from it all. I don't remember her telling me this was a great thing he did or that this was a terrible thing he did, just telling me that it was done. But it was a curious thing; it wasn't a typical thing.

BRIAN

I would have been probably 5. We were about to sit down to dinner. I don't know if I had just been watching television or what, but for some reason I decided we needed a color TV.

I asked Mom, "Can we get a color TV?"

She said, "Well, you'll have to talk to Daddy about that."

So I come into the dining room and he's sitting at the end of the table—we're not underway yet, some people are at the table, others are not there yet.

I said, "Can we get a color TV?"

He said, "No, we really can't, we can't afford one."

"I want a color TV, we need a color TV."

He was trying to tell me how we couldn't get one. Then finally he said, "I'll tell you what, go get your bank."

I had this red-and-black fire hydrant bank that I remember was pretty big, and I went and brought that down. He was sitting at the table in his white shirt and tie—he had come home from work and was still in his business attire—and he leans to one side in the chair and digs into his pocket and pulls out two quarters and puts them in the slot of the bank. And I'm watching this wondering what he is doing.

And he says, "Okay, there, we're going to save for it."

"No! No! That's not what I want. We have to get one right now!"

"No, we're going to save for it, that's what we're going to do."

I got really mad and I said I was going to run away.

And he said, "Well, okay."

So I did. I went in the kitchen and put on my gray jacket and I filled my pockets with Cheerios and came back in the dining room and said, "I'm leaving." And he said, "Okay," and he started to eat. And everybody else at the table started to eat. I think Mom was standing at the kitchen door with her apron on. I looked around and nobody stopped me. So I went out the front door, down the walk, took a left and headed down York Street.

And I started to eat the Cheerios. I crossed the side street and went into the next block and was halfway down that block when I ran out of Cheerios. So I turned around and went home because I didn't have any more Cheerios.

Years later, I learned Mom had followed me from tree to tree to make sure I was all right.

Through it I remember him being calm and deliberate, not persuaded by anything I was doing. He was trying to teach me something, that we could save for it. It would have been good if I had actually caught the lesson.

Chapter 4

MOVING TO CHICAGO

At first, my father started taking trains from Cleveland to Chicago on business trips. He would often leave in the evening. We would sit on the front steps imagining him on a train somewhere in the state of Indiana or moving across a plain of the flat Midwest surrounded by golden fields, the sun setting, reading papers from his briefcase, alone on this thin gray train going to meet other men about business, about changes. Another company was buying out the Magic Chef Stove Company. This meant we would eventually move far away from Elyria.

But now my father was on an evening train to Chicago, and we were getting out of the neighbor's blowup wading pool because the sky was turning black and the air was turning cool and the world seemed oddly still. My mother gathered us up. At first we sat in the living room with flashlights and candles ready. We had never had a tornado before. Where was this train my father was on? Did he know? Was he all right? What might a tornado do to a man on a train, or to us in our white wooden house, my mother and all these seven, eight, nine children? The lights went out. The wind picked up. Everything rocked. The evening grew very black, then silent and yellow. "That's the eye," someone said. Everything rocked and swirled again. My mother led us all down to the basement. Then it passed.

The next morning, we learned that houses had been picked up and dropped on top of cars, trucks had been tossed like toys into trees, roofs were blown off, trees uprooted. Two people were killed up on Lake Avenue only a few blocks away from where we used to go for ice cream; they had been crushed by something. Apparently the train had carried my father away from the storm.

Train trips became more frequent, then plane trips, and finally he was transferred to the Chicago plant. For a long time, he flew back and forth. We would meet him at the Cleveland airport. We'd watch the planes come in, him coming down the ramp with his big suitcase. At home he'd open it up on the living room floor, and it was always filled with Clark bars and Hershey bars and O'Henrys or school tablets, and everyone got to pick.

For eight months from January to August, he lived in a room in Oak Park and took a train to his office in Chicago and came home once a month. My mother learned to drive. She also had a baby in June.

When Eileen was born we did not go to the green to wait. Something was different. She was small. I heard my father on a long distance call saying something about her blueness. Someone at school had told me about blue babies. I didn't know what that meant. All our babies had been healthy, fat, hungry, and pink. There were the usual illnesses and crises, once especially with me at the time of the polio epidemic, but we were okay. There were measles, mumps, chicken pox, viruses, ear infections, colds, infected fingers, but nothing unusual, just the normal things. This was different.

Something was not as it should be.

My father, after visiting with my mother at the hospital where the baby was still in an incubator, gathered us to him around his green leather armchair. All eight of us, small ones on his lap, some on the stool, the rest on the floor. We folded our hands and waited for something important he said he wanted to tell us.

"Kids," he said, "because you have been such good children, God has decided to do something very special. He has decided to send an angel to our house and her name is Eileen." We were in awe of this trust we had all been given, and of his acceptance. In the hospital he sent my mother roses, eight yellow roses and one white rose for this tiny elegant china doll with the fair transparent skin.

To Eileen, Down syndrome is a term like freshman, sophomore, or a job classification. Once, someone said she was handicapped. That upset her. "I'm not handicapped," she said. "I can see. I can hear. I can talk." She knew from school and later work that some kids couldn't see or hear or talk. Others had what she still calls "behavior problems." Even as a young child, she would be the first to comfort them, even if it meant getting them down on the floor to, in her terms, "hug their heads." Every day, she bears out what my father told us about her, this tiny baby who is 56 now. He had foreseen her beauty, watching with my mother from a window high above the green.

Three weeks after Eileen's birth my mother and Cathy went out with my father to find us a house. They found one they liked in a suburb called Elmhurst on a street called York. It was the first house my mother and father had ever owned.

It was red brick with four bedrooms and cost $30,000 in 1958. Just like our house in Elyria, it was right down the street from the church and school so you could, as my parents liked to say, put a slide from our beds right to the school door.

We moved in September over Labor Day, although I did not move with them. I flew up from Alabama with Kevin and Marian where we had gone to spend six weeks of the summer with my Aunt Kay and Uncle Joe while my parents brought Eileen home from the hospital and prepared to move. Three fewer of us made it easier. While we were in Alabama, my father sent us letters he wrote from his room in Chicago. These letters always had words of affection and drawings in them, one drawing for each of us. An ice cream cone for Marian, a gyroscope or something scientific for Kevin, a drawing of a young lady for me.

After six weeks, we were homesick. On the flight from Alabama to Chicago, Kevin got sick in the air sickness bag. I thought it was because he had to sit alone, being the older one of the two little people in my charge. At O'Hare Airport, everything was under construction, and I stood with my little brother and sister, one on each hand, thinking I had gotten off at the wrong place. It was so foreign and vast and I was just 12 years old. Suddenly there was my father with a gang of children.

Seeing him, everything changed.

The towns around Chicago seemed to ring around each other; one became the next suddenly without any country or cows in between, unlike Ohio. Some were congested, like Cicero, with pizza places and neon lights. I don't know if we drove through River Forest or Oak Park that first night, but they were more residential, as were Villa Park, Glen Ellyn, Lombard and Elmhurst.

Elmhurst was green, quiet. There were so many trees. We turned off St. Charles Avenue at a big church onto York Street. My brothers told me this was our street, the main street in town and wider than Dewey Avenue had been, with more cars. It seemed so long. There were big houses on either side, some with wide driveways and long front yards. It was cool, beginning to turn to fall, the trees on either side of the street so tall, the street light lamps like those in history books.

The coolness of the air moved through the car as my father drove us to this new place, where girls on the sidewalks were walking in pairs wearing Bermuda shorts, walking to town or to a dance or some destination that seemed curious and appealing to me. This house on South York Street, this house where my father turned in the driveway, with lights golden through the Venetian blinds of what seemed like a hundred windows, was our house. And inside, my mother and brothers and sisters who had arrived the previous day were waiting to welcome us.

I don't remember gathering our things out of the car or what my father said—maybe "Here we are" or "This is it"— or ever getting out of the car and going in. Just the cool air in the car as we approached, the light from the lamp posts making the young girls more mysterious.

Coming down that street at 12 years old with my father, I had this great sense of expectation and anticipation, a sense that this place was more beautiful and larger and more important than any place he had brought me to before.

Now both of my hometowns are like places in a dream, not really ever there. They are locations on a map I scan for the roads, interstates, highways, cities, states, but can find no way to get there.

Like the photographs of him, black-and-white flat rectangles that bear his resemblance; I study his face, expression, shoulders, tie, waiting for something, listening for a voice. The words Elyria, Elmhurst, Cleveland, Chicago read like distant, exotic places, deep in memory, where life changed; places across boundaries we cannot cross, lines we must always stand on the other side of looking back, like overhearing prayers said by a child whose face is turned.

Dignity

BOB

In Elyria the back of the house had a room that had been added and on the top was a roof that had to be maintained. Dad spent a lot of time working on weekends and was very handy.

So he was up on the roof one day. The kids were playing. The two brothers across the street, Rocky and Jimmy, were tough characters. Jimmy was roughly my age, maybe a year older. We were playing cowboys and Indians. I had a little wooden rifle, and Jimmy just came and took it away from me. I guess I was upset. I was crying.

I said, "Dad, he took my gun."

"Go take it back."

"He's not going to give it back."

"Take it! He took it from you, take it back, it's yours."

That forced me to act. I went to take the gun and of course Jimmy wouldn't give it back, so the next thing I know we're rolling around and it ended up with me sitting on top of him. It was the first time I had been in a fight of any kind.

My mother came out and was horrified at this whole thing. She looked up at my Dad and said, "Why didn't you stop this?"

"Actually, I told him to do it. He's got to learn how to defend himself."

I remember it because he had me do it and it worked, and because he said it was okay to do. The funny thing was, after that those kids gave me a little more respect.

BRIAN

Aunt Anne was working on his car. She was underneath the car and Dad was standing there talking to her. Some friend of his came up and said, "Who's that under there?"

Dad said, "Oh that's my sister."

This was the early 1940s at a time when there wasn't going to be a woman working on a car.

"What, your sister?" He thought Dad was pulling his leg.

And Dad was like, "No, that's my sister."

He said it just like it was the most normal thing in the world. And she popped out from under the car and here indeed she was a woman. She thought that was great. I remember her loving how he was so nonchalant about it. She thought that was cool.

NANCY

Liz [Aunt Anne's lifelong companion] always loved to tell about when Anne had asked her to go out to Elyria to help with the kids when Mom was hospitalized. "I was so tired and Bob came in and he'd have a beer at night and he'd be sitting there when everybody's in bed and he'd say, 'Come on, Liz, have a drink,' and I'd say, 'I'm not a drinker.' But he'd want me to sit down and talk to him. We'd sit there and talk for a long time." She loved that—that he made her feel so nice, so special.

BOB

I was 8 or 9 and was trying out for little league baseball. Back then they had one little league and if you didn't make it you were out. It's not like today with all of the community leagues. I was devastated I couldn't play. I was really disappointed. He said, "Okay, on Saturday mornings we'll have an organized game and I'll be the umpire." He helped me organize a baseball game every Saturday morning. It worked pretty well.

CATHY

Dr. B— said that our youngest sister Eileen should be institutionalized because she was going to drain Mother's energy for the rest of the family. That was the counsel he gave. I remember sitting in the chair just like this when this was being discussed. Eileen hadn't come home yet; she was kept in the hospital partly because she had jaundice and partly because they wanted Mom and Dad to go home and think about this. So it was a huge undertaking. We sat there and they told us all this, and

I said, "Oh no, you wouldn't do that!" and they said, "No, we weren't thinking of doing that," but they wanted to see what we would say, sort of. So we all made the decision together. She was so easy to take care of after all that, you know, she didn't make a peep. Sitting there giving her the bottle took a full 20 minutes.

KEVIN

I was maybe 7 or 8 and I was crying about something minor. Dad said to me, "Save your tears for when they're really needed." He didn't say don't cry or don't be a baby. The message I got was there was nothing wrong with crying, but that it was a serious thing that should be saved for important times.

Chapter 5

ELMHURST, ILLINOIS

Our Elmhurst house had four bedrooms, a bath and a half plus one in the basement, a breakfast room, an alcove for our piano, and a long living room with a fireplace and French doors that opened onto a screened-in porch. From this porch we could see the long backyard with a circular flower bed in the center. Trees shielded one side of the house from the Quigleys' house on the corner. All the way down at the end of the backyard was a stone church that faced the next street, one of eight churches within two blocks of our house.

That first night after we raced up stairways and through the rooms, the brothers and sisters who had arrived before us took us out into the yard where we all stood in the dark, way down away from the house. It was so dark out there, by the alley, the trellis by the garage, the big blacktopped space off the driveway. The blooms from the flower beds seemed only slightly shorter than my littlest siblings, all those dark little bobbing heads out late beneath the sky, all of us safe in the soft dark yard, our parents within.

The next day we took a walk with strollers around the neighborhood up and down the streets with the big houses and the long yards where trees grew across many of the streets, offering arches like passages in a cathedral. Because of their height the sky seemed much further away. It was bright and sunny and spacious and open and green with all those big white houses.

One block over was Wilder Park where someone had given the family mansion to become the Elmhurst Public Library. It had a circular drive and historic rooms that were roped off. The park covered several blocks with tennis courts and greenhouses and a skating pond with a warming house. At age 13 I would read a poem by James Weldon Johnson at the Elmhurst Public Library that began, "And God stepped out on space." Later I discovered that Carl Sandburg had lived on our street and a house had been designed by Frank Lloyd Wright. John Kennedy would come to speak in Elmhurst on his presidential campaign, and his open car would pass down our street. I didn't know all that then, only that things seemed larger, deeper, taller, brighter.

Our house was big and solid, open and expansive but with lots of nooks, crannies and cubbyholes. Lots of entrances and exits, gathering points, stations for dispersal and for boarding again. One of these points was the front entrance hall. Here my father would stand with arms at his side and say, "Okay, who wants to go?" Where didn't matter. Little children would appear, pop out, and race in. Some he'd carry, two would hold onto his belt, and one he'd guide by the hand with little fingers wrapped around his large hand, and the rest would tag along out the door all at the same time, then follow him down the path. And the destination could be near or far, business or fun, it didn't matter. My father's time seemed endless with us, never rushed, as though what he was doing was very important. Time with him had a different meaning.

Returning home we'd climb the gentle slope of the front yard to the porch and stand on the sides of the threshold on tiptoe to look in the high windows beside the door and see my mother coming out from the kitchen, the corners of her mouth turned up. Then spilling into the small foyer, arms, legs, packages, voices, all sticking close to my father like glue, our magnet, all of us coming through the door at once. In the entrance hall we scattered in all directions, like dropped mercury. Straight up the stairs, some turning at the landing, one slamming the bathroom door. A few flew to the left into the living room where the television was switched on and the channels flipped, or to the right into the dining room to a project on the table in some stage of completion. The piano in the alcove would tinkle and a radio could be heard at full volume. The refrigerator door would open and close a dozen times. Things would rustle and whir and sizzle and pop, the phone would ring, and someone would shoot by with a basketball.

My father would stand in the hall while this chemical reaction transpired and tell my mother what had gone on, where we had been, what we had seen, while one little person would run back to pat him or another to say, "Thank you, Daddy," and another to return something my father had given him to hold like his pocket change. Later he'd move about our house room by room, person by person to join in a project here or initiate a conversation there.

At the dining room table he sat for hours bent over the model of the Invisible Man with Kevin. It had transparent plastic skin and all the organs of the human body to scale. My little brother had received it as a gift from Santa. My father seemed to derive as much or more enjoyment as anyone from many of Santa's toys.

In the kitchen, he and my mother had installed a built-in oven and countertop range. This was unusual at the time, a new product he had been experimenting with at work. This left the middle of the kitchen open, so while somebody put away groceries carried in from the side porch, another could stand in the center and talk about everything that happened that day, or roll Cheerios, or race toy cars. You could stop in the half-bathroom that was right off the kitchen if you didn't mind the publicity.

A breakfast room with lots of windows opened to a porch that led through French doors to the living room. This meant we could move from room to room in a continuous circle, rooms opening to rooms, giving a sense that someone you wished to talk to or ask a question of was just in the next room. It provided an endlessness, a continuity, a roundness to life in the house. My father, if not in one room, was perhaps in the next, his voice floating back through the screened porch.

I see my father, standing at the top of the basement stairs saying something with emphasis to a teenager huddled over homework at the kitchen table. Or in the basement hammering, fixing the legs on the coffee table. My father, in the living room, sprawled in his green leather chair, his long legs extended on the hassock, white shirt partly untucked, long arms dangling at full length over the sides, loose, relaxed, his hands open. One hand rising to his neck to loosen his tie in one motion, then hanging at length again, his head back against the chair, so the gray hairs from one of his cowlicks poke up in the back and one unruly strand dips across his brow. About him are strewn newspapers, magazines, things he liked to read. About him, we are lined up on the divan and floor in pajamas watching television.

Then, "Up the golden," my mother says. One, two, three, four, five little bodies would toddle like ducklings up the stairs. The smallest had been carried up earlier. Those older would be nudged up later.

Shortly afterwards my father would go up to say night prayers and make his children giggle quietly, his tall form leaning over their beds, their eyes looking right at him, their Daddy, studying him as I did, saying with him, "God bless Mommy and God bless Cathy and God bless Bobby and God bless Jackie," and on through all of their names, the little ones learning the long prayers of a big family. My father would then help each of them add their private concerns, "God, please take care of us and keep us safe," their eyes illuminated above the animal prints on the tops of their pajamas. Then kisses delivered to warm foreheads, the crib sides squeaking up, my father moving briskly down the stairs to his chair, to my mother.

In our house there was a wealth of time, of space, of possibility. Rooms opened to rooms, scents and voices floated through the open feeling of this house—songs, conversations, plans, television, laughter from a joke, my mother humming, a baby cooing, a baby crying, my father calling, my father in work clothes painting the hall, the fumes, the smoke of his cigarette forming words. With 11 of us, at least 11 different things were always going on simultaneously, more when we brought home our assortment of friends. Someone just bought Boardwalk in the breakfast room. The bathroom pipe broke during someone's shower. Two little ones with the measles are calling my mother from upstairs, my mother answering, my father assisting her.

The sense was of one life together, whole. If one suffered, all suffered. If one triumphed, all did. This feeling would never change. The destiny we formed together in our house would go with us on the first day of the new school year, every new direction. It is what we would always return to, in our marriages, in our jobs, with our children, in all our relationships. We would always remember things that occurred in our house, small moments, details. Like that first night in the backyard, the feeling of safety would return. No matter what, the world could be a place where the love that formed our house would carry us through.

Discipline

BOB

If you got in trouble with Mother, the biggest thing was you didn't want her to tell Dad. I remember a couple of times pleading with her not to tell him. She could be tough, but it would only last for a little while. She would say, "Now you can't go here or do this," or whatever, but within an hour she'd relent. She'd not be mad anymore, she'd relent. But if you told him, he would enforce it.

In Elmhurst, my job was to rake the leaves. We had a lot of trees there, and in the fall the leaves would come down pretty good. I remember one Saturday morning I was getting ready to go to a football game. And he said, "Well you know you didn't do the leaves."

"I'll do them tomorrow."

"No, you were supposed to do them last week. If you want to go the football game you better get out there."

So I'd be out there doing the leaves at 90 miles an hour so I could get to the football game.

Apparently the Eckley strippings were an area near Drifton where they would send kids out to pick coal to bring it to individual houses, to heat the houses. His father had made him work there occasionally. Whenever I would do something bad he would threaten me that he was going to send me to the Eckley strippings.

BRIAN

I did something. I mouthed off to Mom or something. He was mad, he conveyed that. I don't remember him yelling, but I knew he was angry. He told me go up to his room, get his belt, and wait for him. So now I know I'm in big trouble. I pulled the belt out of the closet and I'm standing there holding the belt. And I'm waiting and he's not coming. And I'm waiting and now I'm really getting nervous. And I start to cry and I'm standing there shaking holding the belt. And finally, finally—he timed it perfectly, he knew how long it would take me to work myself up into that—he finally comes in and I thought, "Oh my god I'm going to get whipped with this belt!" He looks at me, looks me right in the eye—"Give me the belt"—now I'm thinking "Oh I'm gonna die!" He takes the belt and he says, "Don't ever do that again. Now get out of here." And I went running out.

JACK

We were playing across the street. I think I was 8 and Sheila was 10. Two neighbor boys grabbed me and they had Sheila come up and tease me. She was swatting me across the face and I wasn't happy. It was aggravating me. But they were enjoying seeing me get aggravated. I was saying, "Sheila, stop it!" Finally they told her to take off, so she starts running because they were going to let me go. But they let me go a little sooner than they should have. Rather than getting mad at them I went tearing after her.

By the time I caught up with her she was on the other side of a car on this driveway, two concrete strips slanting down toward the street. I'm yelling at her and she's taunting me. We're maneuvering and I am trying to get to her. All of a sudden she breaks away and starts running down the driveway towards our house which is directly across the street. I come out from behind the car and catch her pretty quickly, and I take one hand—one hand—and go whack! across her back, and she goes flying. I didn't think I hit her that hard, but partly it was because it was downhill. She goes sprawling and, of course, crying.

At that exact moment, Dad is standing on the porch watching. He has no idea what had happened before. And as soon as she goes sprawling, I hear his voice booming out, "Jack, get over here!"

Somebody ran out and tended to her. She was fine. I think she had a skinned knee or something, but she was fine. Well, by the time I get over there, he is already inside the house. So

I go in the front door and I see him sitting right there. He says, "Come over here," and I go over and he grabs a hold of me, puts me over his knee and spanks me, because he had seen me being completely out of control. And I was trying to protest—"But she was..." He didn't want to hear it. He could see that my response was not proportionate to whatever had happened, and she was hurt. In the middle of this, Mom brings her in and she's moaning and has this big red mark on her back—in the shape of a hand! She had this lily white skin. I was like, "Oh, come on!" And with that Dad goes bam! bam! bam!

Otherwise he never hit me or grabbed me or threw me around or anything else. I think he might have spanked me one other time.

KEVIN

The way that he enforced discipline seemed to focus on certain things. He focused on people not talking back to my mother, or disobeying my mother or giving her a hard time. That was one of his big focuses; he wouldn't tolerate that. He also didn't tolerate kids fighting. Not minor bickering—fighting. I think that has something to do with our family not fighting with each other now. Brian and I fought after Dad had died when we were young adolescents. We didn't get along well for a number of years there. I don't think that would have happened if Dad had still been around, I think he would have definitely put the kibosh on that. Jack and Bob used to fight over the car.

But as adults, as far as I know—I may not know every-thing—I don't think any of us has ever had a fight with another sibling, ever. I'm sure there have been disagreements or what-ever and hurt feelings here and there, but I've never been aware of any sense of estrangement or tension. That's something, considering how many siblings there are and the opportunity for that. As I got older and learned more about people, about all the different kinds of families, I heard so many stories of discord, and I would just scratch my head.

Chapter 6

THE ENGINEER

From our Elmhurst house my father could walk to the train. It was three blocks to the center of town where the tracks crossed York Street with red flashers and black-and-white striped gates that stopped traffic every 30 minutes, more often at rush hour. My father liked trains, so it must have been fun for him to ride them to and from his office in Chicago each day. Most had six or seven passenger cars, silver like our Lionel set. He didn't set up the toy trains at Christmas anymore as he had in Ohio; maybe he was satisfied to ride these real trains instead. Their proximity to our house eliminated his having to drive. It seemed ideal, much more restful for him.

Every day about 7:15 a.m. while we were still lined up for the bathroom, my father would set out for the station. First to the corner, then across the street called Church because five were clustered there, up past the old hotel that was now an apartment building that I visited once when I carried groceries home for an old lady, fragile with lots of big jewelry, up steep steps to a tiny apartment that smelled strange.

He continued up past this hotel and a side street that led to Immaculate Conception Church and School. He'd pass a house with a sweeping porch, the candy store, the bicycle shop, and a place they gave away free light bulbs. At the Sun Ray drugstore tucked in the first floor of the bank, he'd cut across in front of Olswang's department store to the station.

He'd stand on the platform, my father, with his brown briefcase and his newspaper, gazing across the tracks at Fanny Farmer Candies, the Cottage Hill Restaurant and Honey Girl Apparel. Then the train would pull in from Glen Ellyn and he'd get on eastbound for the city. In 25 minutes he'd be at his desk.

One Saturday he took us there. It was a dark red building like a castle with roofs at many levels in the heart of the city. Far within this complex his office was plain, paneled, with a gray metal desk and a basket for mail. There were a few chairs, papers neatly piled and windows that looked out on a shop area. They did research and testing there, with big equipment and large appliances in various stages of development.

He had graduated in mechanical engineering from Pennsylvania State University in 1935 after attending the Mining and Mechanical Institute in Freeland. He landed his first job at the American Stove Company (soon to be renamed Magic Chef) in Cleveland. It was near his older brother Leonard, also an engineer, whom he loved and looked up to. When the Magic Chef line was sold to Maytag, he was recruited as Vice President of Engineering for the Cribben and Sexton Company in Chicago, an erstwhile competitor. At some point after we moved to Elmhurst, Cribben and Sexton was bought by another company, Waste King Universal from California.

His job changed, new people came in, a lot of people were let go. He had to break the news to some of them. My mother said later that this took a serious toll on him. He flew to California, and there was discussion that we might move there. He talked about leaving industry and going into a job with a research laboratory in the city.

But now he was walking to the train early and usually returning home when it had already grown dark.

Intellect

CATHY

He was very methodical. If you said you were worried over this or that, he'd say, "Well now, let's see, let's sit down and talk this over. What would you do if this happened, what would you think about that?" Not that he had a lot of time, but if it came to it he would be very attentive, thinking about what you should do, not dismissive and not grumpy or anything like that ever.

I had a chemistry course in college that I did not like, and he wanted to take the book whenever I wasn't using it, which was most of the time, and he would sit and read that book at night instead of the newspaper sometimes for a long time. He loved all that.

JACK

I remember that Bob and I were thrilled that Kevin came along and got to a certain age. Dad would fix everything just about, and in that house there was a lot to fix from time to time. He needed an assistant, somebody to hold the light, go get that tool, do this, that, and the other. Bob did it at first, but he escaped and I got the job. Dad would be focused and trying to tell me about some of this stuff and I would be looking, going, "Yeah, oh okay. Yeah, I see that," but not knowing what was going on. I remember holding the light and him saying "No over here, over here," and every once in a while he'd get a little impatient because I wasn't holding the light in the right place because I wanted to be outside playing. Somewhere in there Kevin came along, and he was interested in the stuff Dad was interested in. I remember thinking "Okay, I'm out of here—free at last!"

KEVIN

One of the main stories everybody will tell you about me and my Dad is the way I used to help him repair things around the house. That was a relationship I had with him that the others didn't.

I remember one time being down in the basement with him. It must have been Elmhurst. He was fixing the washer and he needed to use his drill. So he asked me to go get the extension cord. I went and got the extension cord, the plug end with the prongs. And he said, "No, get me the female end." And I went and got the female end, the other end, and I said, "Dad"—I was about 7 years old—"Dad, why is this called the female end?" He just broke out laughing, saying, "I'll tell you that someday," and he was just laughing and laughing.

One of the more vivid memories I have of him is sitting on his lap in his chair in the living room and him teaching me math. I remember his whiskers, and his cigarette smell, and him with a piece of paper and pencil. I was probably 7. I was completely fascinated by this stuff he was trying to show me. I think it was a little algebra. He said something about showing me more, teaching me more about it. His manner conveyed the importance of it.

He would bring various interesting things home for me. He brought home a bar of lead—this was before people worried as much about those kinds of things—about the size of a long narrow candy bar and you could bend it with your bare hands. "Look, I can bend a thick bar of metal with my bare hands!" I loved that part of it. The other thing he brought home was liquid mercury in a jar because he thought it would fascinate me, which it did. Every once in a while I'd accidentally spill it, then have to go running after it and suck it all back up into the jar. I had that in my pile of stuff for many years. It slowly disappeared because I kept losing pieces of it. I played with all of his tools for years. His old workbench was my "technical center" from age 8 to 18.

Another time he was fixing the toilet and he had turned off all of the water to the house. I got thirsty and wanted a drink of water. So he got a glass and took water out of the toilet to give to me to drink. But of course he took it out of the tank, not the bowl. But my mother was completely horrified—"You're giving him a drink of water out of the toilet?" He was trying to explain to her that it was water from the tank, which is perfectly clean because it comes up into the tank and is okay to drink. As an engineer it made perfect sense to him. It was a perfectly reasonable thing to do, and I was on his side with that. So I drank the water.

Chapter 7

TURNING AWAY

For some reason, I stopped watching for him to come home. I stopped talking to him about things that happened at school and listened less when he spoke to me. For some reason, I missed opportunities to go places with him, for rides or haircuts or ice cream. Less often did I help my little siblings into the car or shepherd them on excursions. For some reason, when I did I was distant and lost in thought. I'd walk past my father without noticing what color shirt he was wearing or what he was doing or what humorous aside he was making. I'd return from babysitting, see the light in the living room and the light from the television, him sitting there alone, maybe eating peanuts, and call in good night without going to sit with him a while as he often invited me to do, without going in to him to kiss him good night as I had always done before.

I stopped listening for his footsteps in the foyer, for the rise and fall of his voice, the way he'd tell a story, the way he'd put sentences together, the rhythm, the details, my father lifting his hand to adjust his glasses. All of this I'd taken as a given, something to which I could always return.

What I was doing instead I don't remember. I had just turned 14 and started high school. Maybe I was skating with my girlfriends on the smooth circular pond at Wilder Park. Maybe I was moving from place to place with them like musical chairs, looking at bunches of boys with fascination, boys pushing and shoving each other. For some reason, they seemed different from my brothers when they skated into you and made you almost lose your balance. Some of them, usually one, would give you that queasy feeling, like when a boy named James dropped the note on my desk in fifth grade, like that but worse, like something icky and pleasant at the same time.

Maybe I was at Walgreen's drugstore drinking cokes and eating French fries with Pam who wore eye shadow when it first occurred to me that I had a life outside my family, independent, free. I might have been at Mary's or Ellen's birthday party or sleeping over at Diane's or Ann's, who had a pantry and a maid and a swimming pool with a cabana.

On a summer night, I was perhaps at Barbara's or Rita's who lived three blocks from our house and had a screened summerhouse in her backyard. Summer evenings they'd play "Put Your Head On My Shoulder," or "Devil or Angel," and some of the boys would invite girls to dance. I don't recall actually dancing there, rather more the mood of those nights, the possibility that someone might ask me, our faces lit gold from the lamplight.

Being around my father then was like being with a stranger in some ways. Although he had not changed, suddenly there were secret things happening to me, things I didn't under-stand that made me restless and moody, things I couldn't tell my father: menses, bras, stockings, the necessity to wear at least some makeup, all the confusion that made us different from each other in some profound and mysterious way. Some-thing was happening to me that he was not part of, yet tied to in a way I couldn't understand, that made me feel separate and alone. I didn't ask my father's opinion about getting a haircut, eliminating my ponytail. I was around the house less, and when I was, it was in a state of unconsciousness or on the phone or with a bunch of chattering girls.

One night, I left a party in a car with my friends to go to see Gretna, a ghost town outside of Chicago where gangs from the city were said to hang out. Why we would go, one young man's leg in a full cast, I don't know. I told my older brother Bob but not my father. My brother told me how stupid those boys were to take us there, that it was so dangerous, and that we should never do it again. He knew because he had been there himself.

On another occasion, I went over to Rita's house when her mother wasn't home and boys came over and one kissed me. It felt so weird. Walking home, I thought how disappointed my mother and father would be if they knew. It was the betrayal, the breaking of faith that was the worst, doing something that they had told me not to do, doing it to see what it was like, feeling it wasn't worth it, especially how it came between us.

For some reason, I even thumbed my nose at my mother once defiantly while walking down the front walk in response to something she told me not to do. I didn't know what it meant when I did it, but I soon found out from my father. His explanation was as vivid and clear as him telling me at 5, when I had sucked my thumb until it was sore and withered, that if I continued it would fall off. I believed him then and stopped cold turkey. This time, when I thumbed my nose to my mother, his wife, I don't remember exactly what he said or did, as I was too old for a spanking, but he made his point so perfectly clear that I thought it might have been better if my thumb, years ago, had indeed fallen off and disappeared.

I got mad at my father for his regulations and curfews and the "no dates until 16" rule. I didn't understand why he and my mother got so upset about all the kids who had cars, their insistence that we shouldn't be traveling with kids in cars. If we went to the pool or ice pond or a party, we should call them or come home with someone's parents, but not, unless expressly permitted, get in another kid's car and drive around. I didn't understand why he'd wait for my older sister to come home from a date with such attention to his watch. Five minutes in the driveway was okay. Ten minutes was enough. Anything more and he'd flash the porch light until he saw her firstborn face before him.

It was not that we couldn't have experiences or friends; he encouraged us to have fun. But apparently he remembered well about being young and that he too had done things his parents advised against. Apparently he knew that where sexuality blossomed, stupidity was not far behind, that there is a hormonal unconsciousness that kind of sneaks up on a person.

Then there was the boy who started coming to call. He told someone at the pool he liked me and was it okay if he came over. My mother and father said it was, but no dates until 16. We would sit, this boy and I, at the dining room table and not talk, just look out the window or at the tablecloth or study the carpet. He'd lean back as far as he could on the dining room chair, which once suddenly broke and collapsed. I told my mother it was not this burly young man who did it but I, although she never believed me. When he got a new girlfriend, my father overheard me on the phone saying, "Well, he just thinks he's God, doesn't he?" Afterwards, my father stopped me in the breakfast room. "Honey," he said, "if you don't have something nice to say about someone, it's better to say nothing at all. It will hurt them and it may come back to hurt you."

How hard it must be for fathers to let their daughters go through adolescence, abandon them for a while to come back later in a new, deeper way. So much was happening to me that I don't remember, nor did I notice what must have been happening to him, what was developing in his body, invisible to us, silent, cruel, profound.

One morning, we both happened to be going out the door at the same time, I to Mass before school, he to the train. He decided to go with me, spontaneously, as we walked up the street together. It was late for him to be leaving for the office; I don't know why. But we went over to Immaculate Conception Church, he in a gray flannel suit, I in a blue freshman uniform. We sat, just the two of us, in a pew by an open window. The sunlight was exceptionally clear, the air with the sweet smell of fall, perhaps October. My father was on his knees beside me, leaning against the seat, hands extended from long arms before him, the bones in his wrists, hands clasped before him. It's hard to remember the expression on his face or what I was praying for, probably something about liking boys or being in a certain clique, some shallow concern of an adolescent girl. And my father, what were his prayers? What sense did he have of what was coming? Of danger, physical change, pain, worry too deep to say? Or maybe he sensed nothing, maybe he was just asking God to love and care for his wife and for all his little children and for him. We parted in front of the church without knowing.

At Christmas, the boy who "thought he was God" invited me to go the premiere of the movie "Exodus" in Chicago. In my father's enthusiasm and much to my mother's chagrin, he said, "Sure, that's supposed to be a great movie!" He had forgotten I was still 14 and let me go.

Responsibility

CATHY

He worked long hours, always. He never stayed home from work with a cold or stomach flu or whatever. His work ethic was very strong. He always had to be up and out early—"the plant," he had to be at "the plant." On weekends, Mother used to let him sleep in, so we were all supposed to be really quiet. Then when he got up, she made bacon and eggs, always, both Saturday and Sunday, sunny side up. They went to church every Sunday of course. That was a big part of things. Then in the summertime he would do the lawn or take us to the parks. I don't remember either one of them having what we would call pleasure activities. They just worked at raising the children and that was it.

There was no show of anxiety to the children. Even before we moved to Elmhurst and he was going back and forth from Elyria, it was all calm. No one was visiting that anxiety on us. Mother and Dad didn't ruffle feathers until they had to. They didn't transfer all their worries to us. The strange thing was he had this good job, but there was always a narrow margin financially; maybe it was just like that for everybody. But they did have nine children.

Why did they have nine children? When I read some of their letters, it reminds me, they thought of this as a high calling. They didn't think of it as "Poor us" or as "Oh, we're propagating ourselves, filling the world with our kids." It is just that they felt it was what they were called upon to do and they thought of it as a noble endeavor. I do know that they thought of it as a very important wonderful thing to be able to do.

And he always encouraged her that what she was doing was vastly important, and he made this huge fuss over her all the time, thanking her all the time. And when he came home, that was it, he was the center of the universe when he came home. I mean they had a great relationship; I never heard them have an argument. I used to listen at the top of the steps. I didn't want to go to bed with the little kids; I wanted to be with the adults, so I'd sit at the top of the steps just listening to whatever was going on downstairs, whatever they were talking about. Sometimes they would have the TV on, sometimes they wouldn't. They just didn't disagree about anything. That was their quiet time, after everybody went to sleep. That was their peaceful time. I didn't blame them.

I remember buying the house in Elmhurst. He had looked and looked, and finally Mother and I went out and came up with that house. The big focus of where they were going to live was always that it had to have a good school that had to be as close as possible. I remember Dad in the bank, where I assume he had been figuring out what mortgage he could get. He was kind of perspiring, on the phone talking with the sellers, saying okay I've been talking with the bank, so this is how much I can offer you for the house. He was in a phone booth in the bank lobby because that's the way things were back then. He was usually so calm, but now he was very nervous. I never saw him nervous like that except that one time because it was huge, a huge thing to be doing. That was the first house they bought.

It turned out to be a really good house for everybody. I still dream about it for some reason.

BOB

Everybody had a baseball glove. Well I didn't have a baseball glove. You could still play because you'd trade off. The guy in the field would come in to bat and you'd use his glove, but you wanted your own. But they were expensive, and he had all these kids. I remember lobbying for a glove.

So finally he said okay. A baseball glove at that time was maybe 10 bucks. He said, "I'll put half in. You have to earn the other half. Go out and do somebody's lawn or something." So I remember finding jobs to earn the five dollars, then came to him and we went out and got a baseball glove. I think he *could have afforded the 10 bucks. But he was making a point. It doesn't just happen; you have to participate.*

He developed a chart for all of us to do jobs because obviously Mother was overwhelmed with everything. You got so many points for washing the kitchen floor, the bathroom floor, doing ironing, whatever. He assigned the highest number of points to the jobs she liked the least. And the job she liked the least was ironing.

I was probably in eighth grade. I looked at the chart and saw that you got all these points for ironing, more points for ironing than for washing the kitchen floor. I thought, this is easy, so I immediately learned how to iron. That was a good thing because you earned a little money.

MARIAN

There was a squirrel that was getting too close. It was behaving in a way that my father was concerned was rabid. Of course, all of us kids, we were worried about the squirrel. Dad had to call some people to come and take the squirrel or shoot the squirrel. I remember being really, really upset.

And I remember my father; the feeling from him was, "I have to do this, I don't want to do this, but I have to do this." I don't know if I intuitively knew this about him or whether he communicated it, but if he had to do something that was unpleasant or was going to upset somebody he would let you know: "Look,

I don't want to do this but I have to do it." And I've taken that lesson throughout my life. For me, that was probably the first time I ever saw something like that, the bad part of life, having to hurt an animal to protect others. But I remember him not being just like "It's just a squirrel," rather "This is difficult, but we have to do it." And that's what I remember about the event, besides worrying about the squirrel.

BOB

When I learned to drive I was a senior in high school. I turned 16 at the end of the fall semester, so I was getting my license in January of my senior year. By that time everybody in my class had been driving for two years.

He took me out to a big parking lot. He put me behind the wheel and gave me the keys and said now you do this and this. So I did those things. He said, "Now pull over there," so I did what he was telling me.

He said, "Okay, let's go out in the street."

"Already?"

"Well, it's pretty obvious you've been doing this already. This is not the first time you've done this."

"Ah oh, yeah, it's, it's the first…"

"Let's go out on the street. You've probably been on the street before too!"

He was right about all of it of course.

So we pulled out into the street, and it wasn't long before he felt I could go and take my test.

As a matter of fact, I had just gotten my license a week before he died. I remember the night he had the heart attack and they came to get him and take him out. It was snowing. He went in the ambulance. Mother had to get dressed because they had been in bed. Then I drove her to the hospital in the snow. I was uncomfortable with that because I was still a brand-new driver. I think it was the first time I ever drove in the snow.

Chapter 8

JANUARY 1961

My father died suddenly in the middle of the night while we were sleeping.

My mother woke my sister to tell her he was sick and they were taking him to the hospital. Mother came into the room and roused Cathy and I fell back asleep like it was a dream. In the morning, hearing voices in the living room, I called over the banister,

"I'm late for school, Mom. Why didn't you wake me?"

"Come downstairs," she said.

I came down and sat in his chair.

"Daddy died," she said. "He died last night. He had a heart attack. He died at Elmhurst Hospital. They tried but they couldn't save him."

I put my head back. I did not cry. I did not move. I said nothing. I did not know what this meant. At 14, I had experienced death only once removed.

Aunt Sarah, my mother's aunt in Freeland, who was old and gave us lemonade when we visited, had died. We traveled back East, but the kids did not go to the funeral. We stayed at Aunt Sarah's and rocked in her chairs and people took us down the street for ice cream. One of our other aunts had been bright and lively with large blue eyes and blew up air mattresses for us and prepared delicious food when we visited. Later she got something that made her very sick, something we did not understand. One day my father, crying, told us that she had died. And the little sister of Ron, a boy at school, died of leukemia at 5. We went to see her at the funeral home and tell Ron we were sorry. She was wearing a pink dress, tiny and still.

In the middle of the night, my mother said, Dad went into the bathroom and she noticed he was there for a long time. She called to him, but he did not answer. She got up. He was having chest pains. She called the ambulance, woke up my sister to take care of the little ones, woke up my brother to go to the hospital with them. The men from the ambulance carried my father downstairs on a red kitchen chair and put him in the ambulance. My mother and Bobby followed in the car. At the hospital, my father asked Mom to loosen the sheets around his feet at the bottom of the bed. He hated tight sheets around his feet. She loosened them. The doctor came in. They waited outside. The doctor came out. My father had died. It was perhaps 25 minutes, and there was nothing they could do.

About two months earlier, he had had some minor chest pain, angina they said. The doctor gave him nitroglycerin and took an EKG. They said he was okay, no further treatment needed. They didn't even tell him to stop the smoking he had done for about 30 years. That was November 1960. This was January 26, 1961, a month short of his 48th birthday.

On the night he died, my mother said that when she came out of Elmhurst Hospital, a soft fine snow was falling.

There were two funerals: one at Immaculate Conception Church after a wake at Pederson's Funeral Home on York Street in Elmhurst; one at St. Anne's Church in Freeland after a wake at McNulty's on Center Street. In Chicago, my mother sent Jack and me to the shoe store for new shoes.

People brought food to our house, and Mr. Davis, the president of Dad's company, came to the house and held my mother's two hands. Someone from California said that he was the most refreshing person they had ever met. At the first wake, I saw my father there. It was him but it did not seem like it could be him.

A few moments after my father's casket had been carried into the sanctuary, the only sound was 8-year-old Kevin's steps down the aisle. There had been a ruling that the "little kids" were too small to come, so they had stayed at home with someone, but he had, on his own initiative, put on his first communion clothes and walked alone from our house to the church anyway.

My mother and the four oldest children accompanied my father's casket on a plane from the airport where he had met us that first night three years before to Freeland to be buried at St. Anne's Cemetery. At the second wake in Freeland everyone kissed him, as was the custom, unfortunately including me. It did not seem like it could be him.

After the funeral we stood in snow under umbrellas at the place where we brought him finally to rest. It was the same place that just that last August my father had stood with me showing me where the old church and school had been, where he had walked to school as a boy from his house in Drifton. His house was gone now, torn down and replaced by a strip hole, down a road we'd stand on with him each time he'd come home, looking, looking. Just that summer, he had told me how he would come up in the snow through the back gate of the cemetery to school. Now we had brought him back to where he had come as a child to learn.

It had been just last summer, him talking to me. His voice. His tall gentle form. His blue eyes. Him, telling me about his father who had worked in the mines since he was 9, who became the first Irish boss in the region, about his grandfather who had worked in the mines all his life, about himself. How he had a job a couple of summers picking slate at the Eckley strippings. How he hated it. How even when his job got hard now, it didn't seem so bad.

His ancestors had spent their days going deep into the mountains for coal and pay; before that scraping into the soil of Ireland for food; after that earning academic degrees, protection from ever having to go that deep into the earth again, victory over poverty and immigrant status. And going to church, for generations, to rise above human frailty and death and sinfulness and despair, to be christened and confirmed and married, and finally to be given a Christian burial in the same earth they had spent a lifetime trying to escape.

Now only the whiteness. The coldness, the absence, the separation, the loss of him, the cruelty of death, its mystery, its terrible weight. The faces of my smallest siblings looking up at my mother, asking, she looking up higher. Her pain, her strength; at 14 I did not know how deep these went.

For years, the looking for him, the denial, the confusion, the grief would go on. At 14, it was too soon.

Without him, we flew back to Chicago.

Taking Leave

JACK

*There's that portrait of us with the whole family. I'm pretty
sure that picture was taken one or two months before he died
and you can see how much older he looks than Mom, like he'd
gone through a lot. I'm pretty sure that at that point he had
had two heart episodes. I always thought he wanted to have
the picture done then before anything worse would happen.
Of course, he had smoked for umpteen years, and he smoked
Chesterfields, no filter, no nothing. That's just the way it was
back then. He had been smoking for 30 years. The surgeon
general's report didn't come out for three more years.*

BRIAN

*The summer before he died we had taken a trip to see all the
family members. We drove from Elmhurst back to Hazleton
and all up through there and to Philadelphia. At one point he
and Mom flew down to Alabama to see Aunt Kay and Uncle
Joe. She said he was making a point to see everybody and
she said, "I think he knew something then," that he knew he*

was not well. When we visited Aunt Anne, they were making dinner, making mashed potatoes, and she asked him to mash the potatoes, something he would have normally done. But he said no. She always thought that was strange and wondered in retrospect whether he didn't want to exert himself.

BRIAN

In the morning when I would go to school I would get myself all dressed, but I couldn't tie my shoes yet, and I would go into Mom and Dad's room and put my foot up on the bed and one of them would tie my shoes while they were lying in bed and still sleepy. One day I got myself dressed, and I went into their room to have them tie my sneakers and nobody was in there. So I went downstairs and stood at the bottom of the stairs and Mom was coming through the dining room with Cathy and Sheila on either side of her. They were literally holding her up. And I, of course, didn't know what was going on. I looked around, and somebody said, "Daddy died." I went to give Mom a hug—my instinct—and somebody put their hands on my shoulder and held me back. Probably they were trying to save Mom from that and maybe everyone had already been doing that and I was the last one and she had gotten enough. I think in the moment I read it as "Okay, don't do that, don't get emotional," because then I started walking around saying, "See I'm not crying, I'm not crying." I said that several times to show that I could handle it, that I was not going to make things worse. This happened in late January. I turned 6 that March.

Mom told me that some people had advised her that she should send us, especially the little ones, to an orphanage, but she said there was no way she was doing that.

JACK

The morning after he died I came out of my bedroom and I knew something was up, but I didn't know what was going on. I was told what had happened. I guess Mom told me. I remember being upset but not quite grasping what all of this meant at the time. He died—now what does that mean exactly? Whoever had died before that had been more tangential to my life. I remember then having a much better grasp of what it meant at the funeral home, not only seeing him, because it was an open casket, but people coming in to see me, my baseball coach and other people, kids from school. I recall being not quite sure how to manage this in my own head, how to cope with it.

KEVIN

This is not an interesting story from the point of view of what really happened but is an interesting story from the point of view of what I remembered as having happened for many years after his death. The night he died I said good night to him as I always did. I was standing at the bottom of the stairs looking into the living room. He was sitting in his chair watching Groucho Marx. I said "Good night" and went to bed. But for years after that I remembered saying "Goodbye" instead, then correcting myself. I doubt that's what really happened; my memory is probably mistaken.

In the morning when I got up, I somehow sensed that something had gone wrong. This is, I think, an accurate memory. I looked downstairs and saw my brother Bob walk past the stairs with an odd expression on his face. Normally he would have left for school by that time. I was suddenly struck by a terrible thought. I went into my parents' bedroom and knelt down and prayed that my father had not died. I don't know how or why I came to that conclusion. I probably picked up on clues from the nighttime because my father had been taken away in the night. After that I went downstairs and my mother told me the news. To this day I still wonder how I knew while still upstairs, alone.

Chapter 9

NO LETTERS, NOTHING

He did not come back, my father. He went someplace from where he could not return. On a gray train, in his car, on a plane, somewhere we could not accompany him, not to work, not on a business trip. He never returned, not with a suitcase of candy bars or school tablets. He did not turn off Lake Avenue in his Plymouth or turn up our walk in Elmhurst in snow. There were no drawings in letters, indeed there were no letters, no calls. There was no sign of him, no word, nothing but this tall lean aching space in my life.

How impossible to think that my father would not say goodbye, that I would never again see him. It did not seem right. So I would continue to watch for him, in a crowd, in a store, in a circle of strangers beneath a lamplight; and I would continue to hope, believing that my father, the engineer, would surely figure something out.

Within nine months, we moved to be closer to my mother's family, especially to Uncle Buddy, her brother. I would, for a time, receive letters from friends in Chicago, hand-written in white envelopes with my name and new address in black ink, letters I'd shuffle through the mailbox to find when I came home from school, letters I would keep in a cardboard box for years, as if holding these as signs of life with my father. Eventually, news would come that some had married each other and had children of their own, and I would learn the world moves on.

If I could see him now, his long legs striding toward us on some particular morning probably with half a smile at a remark someone made; if I could see him for a single moment, hear him tell us where he had been, what he had done, what he had thought and whom he had met; if he could tell us how he missed us, that he was glad to be home; if I could bid him welcome, even kiss him in a child's way, slide up the firmness of his shoulders, brush the pokey bristles of his side haircut, his whiskers, clasp the back of his neck and pull into him, leaning with abandon against him as once it was great and safe to do, then all this time that he has been gone would be as glacial ice feeding the streams and rivers of a continent. I would let him know how grieved all had been and how much I personally had missed him, how great his absence, how small things seemed without him, how flat, how great on his return.

If for a moment I could see him, my father, standing before me talking, shaping out gears and mountains with his hands, sharing in fellowship with others as he so loved to do, I would look to see if he knew how carefully I followed him, how much I loved him without my saying it, this unspoken language learned by necessity by those who are acquainted with death. It is a language shaped within some private inner chamber where a voice or figure is recognized, as if known through some ancient genetic code.

Me talking to him, him talking to me, in an intracellular place where sunlight is cascading through trees and I am tumbling down a luminous path to a river. And for a moment, if only one, love in one of its divine manifestations opens the ford and I am slowly carried across the water to another shore, surprised and safe with him, beyond the boundary of loss and separation.

Wisdom

BRIAN

For a long time I thought he was this perfect guy and he and Mom were perfect. I still kind of think that because that's all I have, I want to think that. So I think, well, that's probably missing a few pieces. But I have the distinct feeling that he had—I'm not sure the best word to use—class. That he thought more than he spoke. That he didn't say everything he was thinking. That he could handle people. That he was certainly not rough around the edges. That he could get mad. That he could be pretty direct. And that he could be tough on you, but he had that ability to be in a situation with somebody who was being difficult—I don't mean just the kids, I mean anybody—and not let the fact that person was being an idiot or being abrasive affect his behavior. That he would still be under control. And maybe he would decide he was going to let you have it, but the point was he was going to be under control. That was a quality Mom had as well.

So I've been able to get some of his teachings, of his thinking, from Mom. Because I don't know what he thought about a lot

of things, I've started to write what I call "To My Children,"
telling my children what I think about things. Not here's how
to live your life or not that I'm right about everything, but just
here's what I think about various topics and ideas and issues.
All my life I would have liked to know what Dad thought about
a given thing, and I think you always try to give your kids what
you didn't have. There's going to be wisdom a child would want
to get from a father. You might think the same way as him and
not know why. Maybe it's because you heard him say it and
you just don't remember. Somehow he influenced you that
way. I invoke things he said on a regular basis. I use all of it.

One of the things he would say when he felt he needed to
convey that he wasn't going to be a pushover was "Don't mis-
take my kindness for weakness." I think there's a lot of power
in that and a lot of meaning in that. I understand that as the
type of person I am, and I've used it a lot.

We look back on Elmhurst as Utopia, and I always figured that's
not because we didn't have any problems but because we were
little and we didn't know what problems we had. Mom and Dad
had them but didn't tell us. There were money concerns; some of
the letters show that. He was having health problems; we didn't
know about that. She was having health problems; she almost
died from colitis. So it only seemed perfect. It's interesting to hear
that Elmhurst has actually been written about, that it was actu-
ally considered that kind of place by others. It's still a nice place.

Chapter 10

HIM, IN SNOW

One last memory.

When we first moved to Elmhurst, my sister Cathy and I shared the back bedroom over the screened porch. It was blue-green and the closet had a ladder to the attic and a door that went to a balcony. We were never allowed there because it needed new railings.

The little kids shared the front room on the same side. Shortly we switched. They got a linoleum floor with Mother Goose figures and we got the front room that my father had painted peach and where my mother put up white ruffled curtains that had hung in our front window in Elyria.

I read *Jane Eyre* and *Wuthering Heights* in that room, sitting in bed planning for a window seat, looking out at the snow that fell silently beyond white curtains and Venetian blinds. I memorized lines for the drama lessons I took in that room every Thursday afternoon from Mrs. Gapen who taught me at school and offered to give me private lessons because she thought I had potential. I memorized "Giuseppe the Barber" and how to breathe properly, and it was she who gave me the opportunity to read the poem at Wilder Library. For that occasion, my father had taken the whole afternoon off from work.

In that room I spent time listening to a pink radio and wrote a poem on autumn leaves in rain that I submitted to an anthology for kids and read every issue of "American Girl" magazine from cover to cover.

Looking up from reading, the soft snow that fell in Elmhurst seemed different than other snow. It was more white, more cold. Inside everything was warmer. Whatever the snow covered was secret, still. The trees on the sides of the street became shaped with snow, the laden branches almost blocking my vision up York Street to town where sometimes, looking up from my reading, I'd see my father's figure in the falling light, returning from the train, turning up our walk, his hands in the pockets of his overcoat, his footfall on the porch, his feet tramping snow off his boots in the foyer, where my mother's voice and his intermingled.

~

Maybe part of it is that you create what you
want to create. Maybe you impute onto someone
like Dad qualities that aren't there, I don't know.
Because you want that, you want him to have certain
qualities. But then how did you think those up,
as a kid, if they weren't really there?

—Brian

Epilogue

The 6:05 from Chicago

Bob Johnson stepped out of the front entrance of Cribben and Sexton into the dark. The day had been another busy one. There had been a problem with a supplier for the control valve on the most important gas range, and he had spent most of the day on the phone and in meetings. The stress at work had escalated since the merger with Waste King Universal. As executive vice president he had to let a number of people go, some of them his colleagues, many of them his friends. January seemed especially long in Chicago.

He was wearing his long overcoat, a scarf, and a fedora. His hands were bare; he didn't like gloves. He walked down North Sacramento toward the train station. Glancing back he could see the downtown skyline, blue and smoky in the distance across an industrial expanse, the skyscrapers starting to glimmer.

He trudged up the cast-iron steps onto the platform. Others huddled nearby against a wind sweeping in from the city. A faint scent of diesel fuel rose from the tracks but soon gave way to fresher air, probably falling down from above. The sky was swelling with a storm, 12 inches they said, to be added to the couple of feet already on the ground.

The train pulled up. He stepped across the gap into the vestibule and turned left into the car. As he swung his briefcase onto the seat, he felt a familiar burning in his left arm. It slowly spread up to his jaw and nauseated him a little. He paused. After a few moments of trying to will it away, he fumbled for the bottle of nitroglycerin in his pants pocket. He thought it was in the left, but it wasn't—there it was, in the right. He placed a tiny tablet under his tongue.

He understood what this meant. The pain only came now and then, and when he took the nitro it went away. But it kept coming, maybe a bit more frequently now.

The previous summer he had purchased life insurance instead of taking the family on a vacation. He had made sure to visit his mother and his sisters and brother back in Pennsylvania. Last month he had had a family portrait taken, all 11 lined up in three rows, Eileen on Betty's lap, Nancy and Marian in matching floral dresses. Brian had to kneel alongside Nancy and was a little upset because it made him look as short as her.

Bob decided to do something fun with the kids that weekend, to make up for being away at work so much. Maybe go for ice cream or something. He had promised Kevin he would bring home components for the crystal radio project, but he had forgotten again. Must remember next week, he thought.

The nitro had brought on a mild headache, so he slumped against the window and closed his eyes. He let the clacking of the carriage lull him. Soon he was half-dreaming.

He imagined he was headed back to his hometown, Drifton. He found this idea pleasant even though he knew that if he arrived he would find his childhood home demolished and most of the people he had known long gone. But it was still the locus of his oldest memories and of one of the most important events of his life.

One day he took his aunt to the dressmaker. This was a few years after college. He was working in Cleveland but had come back to Pennsylvania for a visit. As he escorted his aunt to the threshold, a girl of 17 with raven hair stepped out from a small courtyard between the shop and the owner's house.

"Hi," he said.

"Hello," she replied.

"Aren't you Betty? I think we met before, but you look different somehow."

"I'm not sure what you mean."

"Well, it's just… it's just that I can't figure out why I haven't paid more attention to you."

She blushed.

"The last time you saw me I was just a girl. Anyway, I've been here the whole time."

So Bob and Betty spent the next three evenings visiting, until he had to return to Cleveland.

He had met plenty of girls in Cleveland. He had no difficulty talking to them, but they were different, cooler than the girls back home. Less open, less trusting. Somehow, he reflected, having more options didn't make it easier to find someone. People seemed preoccupied or distracted by possibilities just around the corner. Or across the room.

The courtship was conducted mostly from a distance, by letter. If Bob was tardy in replying, Betty would match him, and wait before replying herself. She lived with her mother and her mother's family, but her mother had been ill for a long time, so she spent a great deal of time with her Aunt Catherine. Aunt Catherine, though never married herself, had definite ideas about how a young lady should conduct herself when faced with interest from a young man.

Eventually, he proposed, and she called him long distance to accept. In 1940, a long distance phone call often meant momentous news. He had found himself lost for words. The floor of the boarding house hallway where he had taken the call threatened to drop away.

He recalled the rapturous first year, then the first baby and postpartum blur, not long afterwards the second child, then another and another, year after year, now nine in all. Throughout, he and his wife had leaned on each other, and the few times they found no support this way, they fell together until they righted. The children were a gift, and too important for them to fail.

That quiet beauty standing outside her family's shop—it had been so long ago. A moment unbidden, but reverberating still, though more and more as in a dream.

He startled awake as the train lurched to a stop. The car door whooshed open and a spray of snow blew past the opening as he stepped out onto the platform. He felt the cold air in his nostrils. He thought of the house, of the lights within, of the blast of warm air that would greet him when he stepped into the foyer, of Betty in her apron out from the kitchen, of kids running up to greet him.

And he saw that his life was good. That he must throw himself into it and travel through its warmth and its love until inevitably he reached the end.

And with that he held his hat, hunkered down into the blowing snow and headed home.

Acknowledgements

I thank my brothers and sisters who have influenced my life in dimensions too numerous to imagine; their children whom I think of as my own; their loving spouses who are my dear friends; my extended family who lifted us up and carried us through after my father died, especially Uncle Buddy, Aunt Helen, Patricia, Sheila and Bob Boyle; my cousins who were close to my father including the Beckmans; and my other trusted friends who know their special place in my heart.

I would also like to thank Marion Kayhart, Nellie Manges, Robert Coll, Dan Gambet, Mark Arend, Craig Haytmanek, Elizabeth Walker, Carolyn Marino, Martha Herron, Tom O'Leary, and Ed Meehan for their generosity in reading and advising on the manuscript before publication.

Finally, I would like to thank my younger brother Kevin, my editor and "charge," without whom this book would just be a dream.

About the author

E. Sheila Johnson is a graduate of Cedar Crest College, Villanova University, and Bread Loaf Writers' Conference. She lives on a park near friends and family and is part a team working toward the renaissance of a city. Jane Austen, Robert Frost, Emily Brontë, T. S. Eliot, and Emily Dickinson are her favorite authors. She first published a poem in seventh grade in Elmhurst, Ill. about wet leaves in rain.